Kate Boesser

ALPHABIRDS

an Alexander Archipelago Alaskan Aviary

by Kate Boesser

Roundabout Studios

b

B

Blackbird

ALPHABIRDS
an Alexander Archipelago Alaskan Aviary
by Kate Boesser
c2012

Roundabout Studios
P.O. Box 47
Gustavus, Alaska
99826

This book
is dedicated
to my granddaughters,

Layla June
and
Fiona Jane

May birds
fill their lives
with joy.

Austere Auklet sitting proud

A
Auklet

Mama Blackbird and baby below

b

B

Blackbird

Emerald Cormorant catching the sun

Cormorant

Decorative Duck with colors just so

Elegant Eagle with echoing cry

E

Eagle

Fearsome
Falcon
poised
up high

f

F
Falcon

Homespun
Goose
who flies
above

Handsome Hawk down from the sky

h

H

Hawk

Ivory
Gull
as white
as snow

Indigo
Jay
among
the leaves

J

J
Jay

Chattering Kingfisher catching his meal

k

K

Kingfisher

Lustrous
Loon
for now
at ease

L
Loon

Stark
Magpie
in black
and white

Northwestern Crow alighting here

n

N

Northwestern crow

Curious
Owl
opens
its eyes

Polished
Pigeon
preened
with care

Snipe
(called
Quaily)
wings
up high

Grand
Raven
rich
in black

R r

R

Raven

Delicate
Sandpiper
stepping

the sands

S

S

Sandpiper

Fair
Tern
fluttering
fast

Murre
called Uria
firm
and bold

U

Uria (murre)

Varied Thrush with feathers fine

Varied thrush

Stately
Whimbrel
dressed
for show

W

W Whimbrel

Xema
Gull
in grays
and white

Xema (Sabine's gull)

Whimsical Yellowlegs standing tall

Zonotricia
Sparrow
capped
in stripes

Zonotricia (sparrow)

Every
bird
its riches
wears...

Clothes
itself
in color
and light.

ALPHABIRDS
an Alexander Archipelago
Alaskan Aviary

by Kate Boesser

Each bird carved in relief and painted for AlphaBirds depicts a bird that comes each year to the Alexander Archipelago - the island chain that comprises Southeast Alaska. Most of these birds spend time in Glacier Bay.

Author, artist and illustrator Kate Boesser carved the original AlphaBird wood blocks from second-growth basswood from the midwest. Kate Boesser works in her home studio in Gustavus, the gateway to Glacier Bay, where the artist has spent most of her life.

The framed original AlphaBird carvings were purchased through the Alaskan Art in Public Places Percent for Art Program, and hang displayed above the bookshelves at Mendenhall River School on the Back Glacier Loop Road in Juneau, Alaska, near the Mendenhall River and Glacier.

Six carved and painted carvings of Southeast animals by Boesser also hang in the Douglas Library, across the Gastineau Channel from downtown Juneau. A large relief carved panel of wildlife hangs in Harborview Elementary School in downtown Juneau. A number of private carvings, woodblock prints and doors hang throughout Southeast Alaska.

Kate Boesser carves pieces for customers on commission.

kateboesser@mail.com

Made in the USA
Charleston, SC
04 July 2016